BRANSON

MISSOURI

*Travel Guide to
Fun City, U.S.A.
for a Vacation
or a Lifetime*

DAVID VOKAC & JOAN VOKAC

Vokac, David, 1940–
    Branson, Missouri—
    Travel Guide to Fun City, U.S.A.
    for a Vacation or a Lifetime /
David Vokac & Joan Vokac.
p. cm.
Includes index.
ISBN-13: 978-0-930743-27-7
ISBN-10:0-930743-27-X
1. Branson, Missouri—Guidebooks.
2. Cities and towns—Branson, Missouri—Guidebooks.
3. Branson, Missouri—History,
Local.   I. Vokac, Joan, 1948–   II. Title.

Copyright © 2014 by David Vokac and Joan Vokac

All rights reserved. No part of this book may be reproduced in any form, other than brief passages in printed or electronic reviews, without permission in writing from the publisher. Inquiries should be addressed to:

West Press
San Diego, CA
publisher@greattowns.com

PREFACE

Why do we call Branson "Fun City, U.S.A."?

Branson is an ultimate vacation destination for people of all ages and interests. Its attractions are as unique and diverse as you can find anywhere in America. Branson is all about entertainment as its claim to fame. And it does that extremely well. It boasts one of the most impressive live theater strips in America along Country Boulevard. Once known only for country-western, in recent years Branson has matured and now features all genres of music, comedy, dance, and more. A major award-winning amusement park built into wooded landscapes features a naturalized venue for themed and thrilling rides, music, an impressive cave, and artisans working on site. Lake Taneycomo provides all sorts of water recreation including "ducks" (land to water crafts), sternwheel showboat, and excursion vehicles. A downtown mall featuring one of America's most enjoyable water features takes full advantage of its waterfront locale. Other unusual attractions where you can hang, swing, or attempt daredevil stunts abound. Whether it's ziplines or coasters, or museums of all types related to history, natural science, or one-of-a-kind experiences (like a replica of the Titanic), diversions of all sorts flourish.

With its diverse entertainment and recreation base, Branson appeals to people of all ages and inclinations. You would be safe to take your boisterous children, frail grandparents, and finicky friends—they will all find something to pique their interest.

We enjoyed personally visiting every notable attraction, restaurant and lodging in Branson, along with numerous outstanding shows. No business paid to be included. All judgments are ours and are based on our perception of merit alone. We have included more attractions than you can do justice to on a single visit. But once you discover Branson, you'll want to return because there's always more to see, as well as something new to enjoy.

Please visit our website and give us your feedback on your visit to Branson. You can contact us through *greattowns.com* or through our facebook community at *facebook.com/greattowns*.

CONTENTS

Preface	3
Introduction	7
Description	9
History	10
Weather	11
Attractions	12
Boat Rentals	12
—Kayak Branson	12
—Table Rock Lake Pontoon Rentals	12
Boat Rides	12
—Main Street Lake Cruises	12
Branson Scenic Railway	12
The Butterfly Palace	13
College of the Ozarks	13
Dogwood Canyon Nature Park	13
Downtown	14
Food Specialties	14
—College of the Ozarks	14
Fountain at Lake Taneycomo	15
Indian Point	15
Lake Taneycomo	15
Live Theater	15
—Shoji Tabuchi	16
—Yakov Smirnof	16
Mark Twain National Forest	16
Ride the Ducks	17
Shepherd of the Hills	17
Showboat Branson Belle	17
Silver Dollar City	17
Spas	18
—Big Cedar Spa	18
Table Rock Lake State Park	18

Contents

Talking Rocks Cavern	19
Titanic	19
Veterans Memorial Museum	19
Warm Water Features	19
—White Water	19
Ziplines	20
—Branson Zipline and Canopy Tours	20
—Extreme Racing Center	20
—Indian Point Zipline Adventure Tours	20
—Vigilante Extreme ZipRider	20
—Zip Line USA	21
Restaurants	22
Andy's Frozen Custard	22
Big Cedar Lodge	22
Billy Bob Dairyland	23
Billy Gail's Cafe	23
Bradford Inn Eatery BakeShop	23
Branson Cafe	23
Branson Landing	24
Buckingham's Restaurant & Oasis	24
Clockers Cafe	24
Crazy Cajun Citchen	25
Ernie Biggs Dueling Pianos	25
Farmhouse Restaurant	25
Jackie B. Goode's Uptown Cafe	25
Keeter Center	26
Level 2 Steakhouse	26
Ma's Place	27
Mel's Hard Luck Diner	27
Mr. Gilberti's Place	27
Mitsu Neko Fusion Cuisine	28
Outback Steak & Oyster Bar	28
Rocky's Italian Restaurant	28
The Shack Cafe	28
Table 22	29
White River Fish House	29

Contents

Lodgings	30
All American Inn & Suites	30
Big Cedar Lodge	30
Bradford House	31
Bradford Inn	32
Branson Towers Hotel	32
Branson's Best	32
Castle Rock Resort & Waterpark	32
Center Pointe Inn - Best Western	33
Chateau on the Lake Resort Spa	33
Clarion Hotel at the Palace	33
Comfort Inn & Suites	33
Grand Country Inn	34
Hilton Branson Convention Center	34
Hilton Promenade at Branson Landing	34
Hotel Grand Victorian	35
Keeter Center	35
Lodge of the Ozarks	36
Radisson Hotel Branson	36
Rock Lane Resort & Marina	36
Savannah House Hotel	37
Scenic Hills Inn	37
Still Waters Lakefront Resort	37
The Stone Castle Hotel & Conference Center	38
Welk Resort Branson	38
White River Lodge	38
Basic Information	39
Livability	40
About the Authors	42
Index	43

INTRODUCTION

This book uses the same format and conventions from the comprehensive national guidebook, **The Great Towns of America**. For the convenience of anyone not familiar with that book, here is an explanation of the meaning of the book's major elements.

Weather Profiles: the "Vokac Weather Rating"
The "Vokac Weather Rating" © (VWR) is a unique feature of all "Great Towns" guidebooks. It measures the probability of "pleasant weather" (warm, dry conditions suitable for outdoor recreation in light sportswear). Average high and low temperatures, rainfall, and snowfall for each month are also provided. A proprietary algorithm is used to rate each month's weather from "0" (intense weather requiring related suitable clothing) to "10" (ideal). Every increment of one on the VWR scale represents a 10% greater chance of pleasant weather. Generally, ratings of "7" or above indicate a high probability of desirable conditions for outdoor activity.

Locations, Ratings, Prices
Branson has a delightful historic downtown plaza and all mileage and directions (N, S, E or W for North, South, East or West) are calculated from that central point. In terms of ratings, every effort was made to include all of the places that the authors believe best convey the charm of Branson. In addition to resorts, bed-and-breakfasts, and lodges, the best hotels and motels of major chains are included. Desirability of each facility can usually be discerned from each review's length. Comparable information is provided about the relative quality and cost of every restaurant and lodging.

Restaurants
The basic price information reflects the cost of an average dinner (soup or salad and entree) not including tip, tax, or beverage. Categories and related prices are: Low: under $12; Moderate: $12–$24; Expensive: $24–$36; and Very Expensive: $36+. Meals that are served are indicated as B (breakfast), L (lunch) and D (dinner).

Introduction

Lodgings
Comparisons of costs were for high season weekend rack rates apart from discounts, seasonal variations, and local taxes. The categories for nightly costs are: Low: under $75; Moderate: $75–$150; Expensive: $150–$300; and Very Expensive: over $300.

Livability of Great Towns
Most visitors are attracted by the many natural and cultural charms of Branson. Beyond these, for those contemplating relocation, the final chapter provides data on some of Branson's key quality-of-life indicators.

Some Final Comments
All information has been carefully checked, and is believed to be current and accurate in 2014. No malice is intended or implied by the judgments expressed, nor by the omission of any facility or service from this book.

This guidebook is unusual in these ways:
(1) The authors personally visited all features, and have distilled them to include all of the authors' determinations of the very best.
(2) No business paid to be included in this book, and no advertising was allowed.
(3) Websites for businesses are always included when available.
(4) All material is consistently arranged in a simple, uniform layout that makes it easy to use.
(5) The quality of weather is rated for each month in Branson on a zero-to-ten scale using the copyrighted © Vokac Weather Rating.
(6) Livability factors comparing Branson to major cities and America as a whole are summarized.

DESCRIPTION

Branson is the recreation and entertainment capital of America's heartland. Gentle woodlands and folds of the Ozark Mountains surround the choice locale along the picturesque banks of a historic stream and reservoir. One of America's most glittering arrays of live entertainment showplaces lines "The Strip" for miles west of downtown. Name acts headline elaborate theaters with music and comedy styles that appeal to all ages and tastes including an increasingly international audience.

Outdoor recreation opportunities are abundant in the expansive lakes and sylvan hills and hollows of the Mark Twain National Forest which surrounds town. In town, Lake Taneycomo provides walkways, boat rentals and rides. One of Branson's distinctive options is a tour on a "duck boat," an amphibious land-and-sea vessel which flops into the water after its road tours.

The volume of tourists has attracted a diverse range of museums, many housed in dramatic structures. Along the 76 Strip, the landmark Titanic replica is a full half-size of the original ocean liner with a fascinating tour that puts you on board the doomed vessel. Nature lovers will adore the hands-on Butterfly Palace; patriots shouldn't miss the Veterans Memorial Museum; and thrill-seekers have a choice of amusement parks, water parks, zip lines, and much more.

Traditional Ozark arts and crafts are abundantly available. In Silver Dollar City, permanent booths along a scenic walkway allow you to interact with craftsmen at work, buy and order art objects, taste local products, and listen to all sorts of live music.

Restaurants and lodgings are abundant, generally well-priced, and range from basic to imaginatively and romantically themed.

HISTORY

Branson was named in 1882 when Reuben Branson opened a general store which served as the post office. A relatively mild four-season climate, clear streams and lush forests made this area popular with homesteaders in the 1880s. By the early 1900s, travelers began coming to enjoy the landscapes and fishing, especially following the popular book about this area published in 1907, *The Shepherd of the Hills*, and Powersite Dam, built in 1912 to create Lake Taneycomo which frames Branson to this day.

Tourism was already popular when the Marvel Cave was opened to paying visitors in 1894. The caverns were eventually modernized with walkways and lights, and soon thereafter, the land above the cave was developed as a frontier-town-styled amusement park. Carefully woven into the Ozark landscape, Silver Dollar City has grown with nearby Branson's increasing popularity into a major amusement park featuring rides, music, and working craftsmen.

After World War II, Branson started a growth spurt, particularly attracting artists and craftsmen drawn by the unspoiled beauty of the Ozarks. The first theater opened in 1959—the Baldknobbers' hillbilly show. Throughout the 1960s, theaters began locating along Highway 76, all with Ozark Mountain-style country/western music and humor which initially set the tone for the town.

By the 1990s, more diversified talent made Branson their homes and established permanent theaters. Today, the sophistication of theaters with terrific acoustics, the talent and imagination of performers, and the range of shows rival New York, Las Vegas and other top venues. Yet, show prices and surprising accessibility of performers to their audiences remain unaffected by the growing fame of the town.

Other forms of entertainment have become as diverse as the theatrical offerings. In addition to water-oriented recreation on Lake Taneycomo and Table Rock Lake, there is a wealth of museums covering everything from butterflies to veterans. Silver Dollar City is a world-class family attraction. As a recent bonus, the downtown shopping plaza, Branson Landing, draws crowds for its free fountain-and-fire show that dazzles onlookers hourly.

WEATHER

Branson has a traditional four-season climate. Occasional rainfall is fairly consistent throughout the year. Spring showers from April through June set the stage for summer flowers. July and August are the warmest months, with high humidity adding to the perceived hotness. The most pleasant weather occurs in fall when leaves are turning and the temperature ranges are pleasant. Autumn at Silver Dollar City is not to be missed, with the sounds of music and crunch of fallen leaves adding to the magic. Winters are moderately cold, with both rain and snow, but relatively short. Even with the onset of winter, December is a busy month with spectacular Christmas shows attracting aficionados here to get into the holiday spirit.

Branson, Missouri Vokac Weather Chart

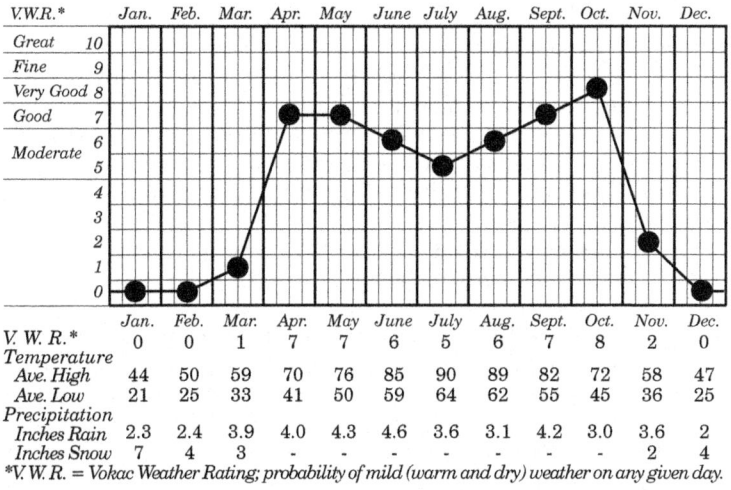

	Jan.	Feb.	Mar.	Apr.	May	June	July	Aug.	Sept.	Oct.	Nov.	Dec.
V. W. R.*	0	0	1	7	7	6	5	6	7	8	2	0
Temperature												
Ave. High	44	50	59	70	76	85	90	89	82	72	58	47
Ave. Low	21	25	33	41	50	59	64	62	55	45	36	25
Precipitation												
Inches Rain	2.3	2.4	3.9	4.0	4.3	4.6	3.6	3.1	4.2	3.0	3.6	2
Inches Snow	7	4	3	-	-	-	-	-	-	-	2	4

*V. W. R. = Vokac Weather Rating; probability of mild (warm and dry) weather on any given day.

ATTRACTIONS

The reason Branson is one of the nation's top travel destinations is its quantity and variety of things to do. It has become the nation's most complete source of attractions and diversions for entertainment, education, and both natural and manmade forms of recreation. No matter what your age, physical condition, or interests, there is something for everyone to enjoy in and around Branson.

Boat Rentals
  Kayak Branson   *(417)336-2811*
  12 mi. SW at 5403 State Hwy. 165
  kayakbranson.com
Single, double or triple kayaks or canoes or stand-up paddleboards can be rented for on-your-own or guided trips to appreciate the beauty of Lake Taneycomo or Table Rock Lake. They also provide shuttle service if you have your own watercraft.
  Table Rock Lake Pontoon Rentals   *(800)662-9984*
  18 mi. W at 318 Nautical Circle - Kimberling City
  pontoonrentals.com
Pontoon boats that are 24 feet in length and equipped with on-board barbecue units are available to enjoy on Table Rock Lake which has more than 750 miles of shoreline to explore. The operators are very flexible on how long you rent the boat, and also allow you to dock it at your area lodging.

Boat Rides
  Main St Lake Cruises   *(417)239-3980* *(877)382-6287*
  downtown at 7 N. Boardwalk
  mainstreetlakecruises.com
See another side of Branson from Lake Taneycomo's 100-foot-long luxury yacht that shows off everything from wildlife to a waterside view of the memorable Fountain. Cruises in the morning, dinner, and sunset capture different perspectives on the beauty of the Ozark environment.
  Branson Scenic Railway
  (417)334-6110 *(800)287-2462*
  downtown at 206 E. Main St.
  bransontrain.com
For a scenic and sentimental journey, the nearly two-hour trip that leaves the historic downtown depot several times daily is a winner. Restored Vista-Dome and other posh passenger

Attractions

cars provide plush comfort, or coach seating, for a narrated forty-mile round-trip through otherwise inaccessible foothills and river valleys. In addition to two to five excursions daily from mid-March to late December, there is a dinner train ride from April to the first week in November.

The Butterfly Palace *(417)332-2231*
  4 mi. NW at 4106 W. 76 Country Blvd.
  thebutterflypalace.com
The Butterfly Palace and Rainforest Adventure is a delightful post-millennium showcase where the whole family will be enchanted by artistic displays intended to give people interactive proximity to a myriad of butterflies. You will get up-close and personal—with patience and luck, you'll have a colorful flying friend land on you during your visit. Don't miss the fifteen-minute 3-D film, a first-class combination of education and beautiful photography. You can also lose yourself in the Emerald Forest Mirror Maze, and move on to the Insect Zoo. Open year-round from 9:00 to 5:00 daily.

College of the Ozarks *(417)239-1900   (800)222-0525*
  4 mi. SW via US 65 at 1 Industrial Pl. - Point Lookout
  cofo.edu
Students work, rather than pay, for their education in this extraordinary small liberal arts college. All of the 1,400 students work 15 hours a week during the semester and several 40-hour workweeks each year in jobs starting with mowing lawns, milking cows or waiting on tables and progressing to jobs with substantial responsibility that will provide work experience as well as allow them to graduate debt-free. The **Ralph Foster Museum** features Ozark-area memorabilia. A reproduction of a historic water-powered grist mill produces whole grain meal. The handsome campus also houses a weaving studio, store, jelly and fruitcake kitchen, and student-run restaurant and lodgings (see **Keeter Center**).

Dogwood Canyon Nature Park *(417)779-5983*
  26 mi. SW at 2038 W. Highway 86 - Lampe
  dogwoodcanyon.org   (800)225-6343
Some of the most beautiful scenery in all of the Ozarks is now fully protected in Dogwood Canyon Nature Park. All sorts of outdoor adventures can be enjoyed in 10,000 acres of pristine canyons, hills, and meadows accented by tree-shaded streams, ponds and waterfalls. A clearly-marked trail

Attractions

extends for four miles each way up Dogwood Canyon which is appropriately named for spectacular white clusters of flowers in fullest bloom in spring. All sorts of attractions like hand hewn bridges, a wilderness chapel, caves, and rock shelters with human remains dating back nearly 8,000 years line the trail along with numerous pools full of trout (enjoying the 57° spring water). Highlights include several waterfalls seeping from high limestone cliffs. Visitors can enjoy walking and all sorts of guided tours by bicycle, segway and horses. The tram tour that leaves several times daily goes the whole distance, and jeep tours are narrated. Half-day guided catch-and-release fly casting trout fishing is popular. Perhaps the most unique adventure is a horseback ride for four guests to join cowboys for a cattle drive of a small herd of Texas longhorns. The **Canyon Cafe** (L only—Moderate) has a limited menu highlighted by bison raised here and there is an adjoining general store. Cozy authentic log cabins with a covered deck, wood-burning fireplace and full kitchen are also available to extend your stay.

Downtown

Part of Branson's appeal is this highly walkable district featuring all major elements of good urban planning in the key retail district by the lake. Amenities include a lot of street furniture plus sculptures and floral displays; free public toilets; a large free parking lot; no parking meters; and a free trolley. In addition, occasional free entertainment is encouraged with sidewalk musicians displaying the kind of talent that may ultimately lead to professional performances in Branson's theaters.

Food Specialties

College of the Ozarks *(417)690-3395*
4 mi. SW via US 65 at 1 Industrial Pl. - Point Lookout
http://images.cofo.edu/cofo/fruitcakeprd.pdf

As part of their education, students learn how to make fruitcakes, nearly two dozen kinds of canned preserves, milled grains, and honey products. Many source ingredients are grown on campus, and all are carefully tended under expert guidance. They compete favorably with commercial brands, and are available through either mail order sales or at the Keeter Center gift shop as well as elsewhere on campus. By purchasing these products you can both enjoy the tasty treats and help support their educational programs.

Attractions

Fountain at Lake Taneycomo
downtown at Branson Landing
The "Wet Design" group of Las Vegas Bellagio fame has taken water and fire to new heights in a magnificent tribute to "the new" Branson. Water geysers up to 120 feet high, huge fire cannons, intense strobe light, and resounding music combine full force at the top of each hour from noon til late evening (including scheduled special shows) to wow audiences assembled to enjoy the free show. Lake Taneycomo and the heart of Branson adjoining the fountains provide an ideal backdrop.

Indian Point
11 mi. W via W. 76 Country Blvd. & Indian Point Rd.
If you want a tranquil lakeside getaway, this four-mile-long peninsula has many miles of shoreline with a wealth of water-related boat rentals, dockage, and moorage. Swimming is also popular. Jump in anywhere, or at the one designated beach. Lodgings from rustic cabins to contemporary condominiums and restaurants are located all around the lake.

Lake Taneycomo *(417)334-3015*
downtown on Lake Dr.
Missouri's first major manmade lake (1913) extends more than twenty miles below Table Rock Lake. A scenic park lines the reservoir's banks downtown. There are numerous facilities for fishing, boating, and camping. At Branson Landing boardwalk, boat rides, rentals, and fishing excursions can be arranged.

Live Theater
W of downtown, primarily along W. 76 Country Blvd.
Diverse venues offer all styles of shows, ranging from state-of-the-art theatrics to the homespun country/bluegrass/comedy that originally made this a famous district. The live theaters lining the main thoroughfare reflect the power and glory of a top American entertainment town. Many, like the Moon River Theater, have outstanding acoustics. As a bonus, nationally famous stars frequently perform throughout Branson on tour. Tributes to "the greats" from a bygone era abound, including a delightful Elvis; the Liverpool Legends managed by George Harrison's sister; and Dolly Parton's majestic theater. Contemporary and innovative shows include "Six" (human voices that sound like instruments). Book popular venues in advance. Among many outstanding options, the authors' favorites are:

Attractions

Shoji Tabuchi
(417)334-7469
4 mi. NW at 3260 Shepherd of the Hills Expy.
shoji.com
One of America's most legendary live shows has been running continuously in Branson for more than twenty years. Shoji's remarkable talent and versatility, along with his engaging smile and manner, quickly win the audience to his performances that include classical, country/western, rock and roll, movie melodies, and always include a patriotic note. Dorothy and Christina Tabuchi add appeal as well, as do Shoji's frequent captivating costume and set changes. The plush 2,000-seat theater features one of the country's best systems for displaying sights and sounds from romantic to hyper tech. As an added attraction, the gentlemen's and ladies' bathrooms are destinations worth exploring (and are among the most photographed bathrooms anywhere). Shoji Tabuchi is Branson's premiere not-to-be-missed show. Plan ahead because Shoji sometimes goes on tour.

Yakov Smirnoff
(417)336-3838
1 mi. N at 470 State Highway 248
yakov.com
In 2014, you can see this legendary comedian at his dinner show in his theater from October through December. The unique view of America from Yakov's perspective as a Russian immigrant is as endearing as it is funny. Yakov captures the humor of life and transitions easily into a moving tribute to America through sharing his personal story and heartfelt love for our nation (of which he is now a proud citizen). The result is America's most uplifting patriotic show. The well-choreographed production ranges from Yakov's clever monologues to his more serious thoughts on relationships gained from his degree in human behavior coupled with his inherent observational skills. The classy theater works well to showcase (for more than twenty years) Yakov's remarkable talent both as a performer and as an artist.

Mark Twain National Forest *(906)428-5800*
  surrounding town
  fs.usda.gov/mtnf
This Missouri national forest is a classically Ozark blend of Eastern forest and Western desert habitats, home to

Attractions

fascinating creatures like eagles, roadrunners, armadillos, and wild turkeys. In addition to abundant hiking and camping opportunities, the North Fork River, fed by nine major springs, offers limitless adventures for canoeists and fishermen. Many outfitters serve the national forest.

Ride the Ducks   *(800)987-6298*
2 mi. W at 2320 W. Hwy. 76
ridetheducks.com

Climb aboard a restored World War II amphibious vehicle (a "duck") for a narrated land and lake excursion. Lots of laughs and information enhance the narrated hour-plus tour in a multifunctional vehicle that traverses city streets and then splashes into the lake to do double-duty as your water vessel. Open March through November.

Shepherd of the Hills   *(417)334-4191   (800)653-6288*
7 mi. W at 5586 W. 76 Country Blvd.
oldmatt.com

For a break from the action in Branson, you can slow down at Shepherd of the Hills, an old-fashioned themed tourist stop based on Harold Bell Wright's novel of the same name. Several vintage buildings of the era involving Wright and his characters are stops on a tram tour of the ridgetop site. For additional fees, there is also a dramatic 230-foot lookout tower with a 360° walkaround at the top with fine Ozark outback views on a clear day and a zipline (see listing).

Showboat Branson Belle   *(417)336-7100   (800)987-6298*
9 mi. SW at 4800 Hwy. 165
showboatbransonbelle.com

A mighty sternwheeler offers a scenic two-plus-hour cruise of Table Rock Lake, with lunch or three-course dinner and a rollicking live show, plus sightseeing along the picturesque reservoir.

Silver Dollar City   *(417)336-7100   (800)831-4386*
9 mi. W at 399 Indian Point Rd.
silverdollarcity.com

Silver Dollar City is one of America's best theme parks. An 1890s-style Ozark settlement shares an expansive site full of towering trees and colorful gardens with numerous stages and theaters. There are more than thirty major thrill rides and attractions as scenic as they are exciting. "Outlaw Run" won the Golden Ticket award for the "best new ride" for theme parks worldwide. More than a hundred resident

Attractions

craftsmen demonstrate traditional artistry from wood carving to glass blowing, and a "culinary and craft school" instructs visitors about country crafts and cooking. Comedy skits and country bluegrass, gospel and Dixieland music are performed throughout the park in more than forty shows daily. The year 2014 features a year-long celebration of America. The largest theater is the 3,000-seat Echo Hollow Amphitheater. Several major festivals are also held here annually, including the rollicking bluegrass and barbecue festival in the spring, and the festival of American music and crafts in the fall. Under Silver Dollar City is **Marvel Cave**—the original attraction dating back more than half a century. A highlight is an enormous twenty-story-high "room." Open March through December.

Spa
  Big Cedar Spa   *(417)335-2777   (800)225-6343*
  10 mi. SW at 612 Devil's Pool Rd. - Ridgedale
  bigcedar.com
Rejuvenation, inspiration, and well-being through relaxation therapies are the goals at Big Cedar Lodge Spa. The new (in 2014) 18,000-square-foot world class facility features treatment rooms with fireplaces, an indoor grotto pool, and an ice room. Treatments include facials, manicures, pedicures, body wraps, body polish, and a wealth of different massage treatments. Especially distinctive are couples' massage classes where each participant receives massage and has the opportunity to work hands-on with the therapist to massage their partner. The Signature Spa Package includes a body polish, one-hour Swedish massage, and a nourishing body wrap.

Table Rock Lake State Park   *(417)334-4704*
  9 mi. SW at 5272 Hwy. 165
  mostateparks.com/park/table-rock-state-park
Bass, crappie, and walleye fishing are popular in Table Rock Lake. So are swimming in relatively warm areas near shore, plus scuba diving, boating, and water skiing. Pontoon and power boat rentals are available at State Park Marina (stateparkmarina.com, (888)993-2628) from March to October as well as fishing boats and guides, plus numerous camping facilities.

Attractions

Talking Rocks Cavern *(417)272-3366*
13 mi. NW at 423 Fairy Cave Ln. - Reeds Spring
talkingrockscavern.com
Guided 50-minute walks on pathways reveal colorful living crystal formations in one of Missouri's prettiest caves. Open daily 9:30 a.m. until 5 or 6 p.m. While you're there, enjoy the outdoor bird show at **Wings of the World** [(800)600-2283], an interactive exhibit featuring over 500 birds from more than 85 species. You can hand-feed the birds and/or watch a show in their amphitheater.

Titanic *(417)334-9500   (800)381-7670*
4 mi. W at 3235 W. 76 Country Blvd.
titanicbranson.com
The front half of the doomed ocean liner, the biggest in the world of its time (1912), looms high above the adjoining strip in a half-scale replica. Hundreds of authentic artifacts are on permanent display along with dramatic movies and recent video from the probe of the ship's contents. You can explore the grand staircase, the captain's bridge, and gallery that tells the tales of child passengers, plus many other poignant exhibits. Open year-round.

Veterans Memorial Museum *(417)336-2300*
1 mi. W at 1250 W. 76 Country Blvd.
veteransmemorialbranson.com
With more than two thousand items, veterans of all twentieth-century wars in all military branches are honored. The world's largest bronze memorial sculpture (of 50 life-sized WW II soldiers storming a beach) is the centerpiece. You will leave with a heightened appreciation for the men and women who have served our country so valiantly

Warm Water Feature
  White Water *(417)336-7100   (800)831-4386*
4 mi. W at 3505 W. 76 Country Blvd.
silverdollarcity.com
A 500,000-gallon wave pool, water slides and flumes, inner-tube rapids, lazy river and pools are highlights of the area's most elaborate water park. The biggest thrill in the attraction's history—"Kapau Plummet"—opened in 2014 with two 240-foot dueling slides featuring a 70-degree encapsulated plunge slide. In peak season, Thursday nights include a "dive-in" movie. Open mid-May to mid-August plus weekends through the end of August.

Attractions

Ziplines
As new forms of entertainment take hold, you can bet that Branson will find a way to provide them. Not surprisingly, many new zipline adventures have found a home here, including:

Branson Zipline and Canopy Tours *(800)712-4654*
8 mi. N off Hwy. 65 at 2339 U.S. 65 - Walnut Shade
bransonzipline.com
Located in the Wolf Creek Preserve, great care was taken to create a zipline experience that minimized the impact on the surrounding natural setting. You have a choice of three trips (ranging from 1.5 to 3.5 hours) which include both ziplines and "sky bridges," and the most adventurous one includes a freefall. The beautiful natural setting can also be enjoyed on foot on a leisurely guided (downhill) tour. Grounds include observation decks, a snack area and a major gift shop. Ideally you would book the zipline adventures in advance. Open March through December.

Extreme Racing Center *(417)239-2947*
5 mi. W at 3600 W. Highway 76
You can choose to lie, stand, or sit on a flying surfboard for a five-minute half-mile ride that travels up to thirty miles per hour. Open March through December.

Indian Point Zipline Adventure Tours *(417)338-3339*
10 mi. W at 1056 Indian Point Rd.
indianpointzipline.com
Starting out high on a forested hill in the high country above Branson is a first-rate zipline adventure that lasts a little more than an hour. During that time you will sail among and above the trees for a distance of more than half a mile at speeds as much as forty miles per hour. There is only a single tower to climb for the whole trip. New in 2013 is the Indian Point Hydro Slides where you can wear your swimsuit and take a mat down a hill for hundreds of feet. The facility also includes a cozy short-order cafe.

Vigilante Extreme ZipRider *(417)334-4191*   *(800)653-6288*
7 mi. W at 5586 W. Highway 76
vigilanteziprider.com
This is a scenic and exhilarating ride that doesn't involve much effort. You take a glass elevator up to the top of Inspiration Tower. Then you launch from the open-air observation deck which stands 230 feet above one of the highest points in

Attractions

Southwest Missouri. Guests are carried downhill in a special chair-like harness (weight range 75 to 275 pounds) at speeds up to fifty miles per hour for the half-mile ride of scenic tree-shaded hills and dales in and around the Shepherd of the Hills entertainment center. The rider has no control of speed or braking; the trolley does it all. Riders are brought back to the starting point by tram or jeep.

Zip Line USA *(417)559-5398   (417)272-1600*
18 mi. NW at 3335 US 160 - Reeds Spring
goziplineusa.com

The longest trip (two hours-plus) travels more than three miles at heights up to 350 feet above ground through a canopy of massive shade trees. There are no towers to climb. Just a few stairs reach nine ziplines and sky bridges. Several shorter trips are also available, and there are night trips too. Open April through September.

RESTAURANTS

While Branson has many restaurants oriented toward families, options are expanding in recent years with some nods to gourmet diners. Prices tend to be surprisingly reasonable, and dress code is casual. Most restaurants are happy to accommodate showtime constraints.

Andy's Frozen Custard   *(417)337-5501*
  4 mi. W at 3415 W. 76 Country Blvd.
  L-D.   *Moderate*
  eatandys.com
Andy's Frozen Custard (made fresh hourly) is a real winner. Treats like blueberry or triple chocolate concrete and all kinds of other specialty concretes, sundaes, malts, shakes, freezes, and more are served along with two dozen kinds of toppings. The big snazzy 1950s-retro ice creamery provides a choice of window or drive-in service.

Big Cedar Lodge   *(417)335-2777*
  10 mi. SW (via US 65) at 612 Devil's Pool Rd. - Ridgedale
  B-L-D. Sun. brunch   *Moderate–Expensive*
  bigcedar.com
Big Cedar Lodge, the Ozarks' premier resort, prides itself on fine cuisine as well as memorable settings. The **Devil's Pool Restaurant** (B-L-D. Sun. brunch) features regional specialties like smoked trout or prime rib given careful attention with housemade sauces, baked goods and desserts. Rustic elegance is marked by a huge stone fireplace, bark-covered pine beams, exposed log rafters and oak plank floors. Trophy animal and fish mounts and classic sporting gear adorn the walls, and picture windows frame a forested lake beyond an umbrella-shaded dining deck above Devil's Pool. The stylish **Truman Coffee & Cafe** features pastries baked fresh daily and lighter fare to go or to enjoy on a large lovely patios, one overlooking a picturesque arm of Table Rock Lake, or in a 1920s Tudor-style cottage. In **Worman House** (D only. Sun. brunch—Expensive), classic Continental and American specialties are given expert attention using top-quality fresh ingredients of the region where possible. Consider a pan-roasted Ozark trout with roasted almond pan sauce or pork chop glazed with local honey. Luscious desserts are also made here, for example, gooey butter cake with salted caramel ice cream. The casually elegant decor is in the spirit of the

Restaurants

1921 manor house in which it is located. There is also live entertainment. The **Buzzards Bar** (L-D) features specialty drinks and light selections from the Devil's Pool Restaurant (like the signature salad with blueberry-poppy seed dressing) along with nightly entertainment. A new-in-June-2014 fine dining venue is **Top of the Rock Restaurant** overlooking spectacular views of the lake and forested hills.

Billy Bob Dairyland *(417)337-9291*
3 mi. W at 1901 W. 76 Country Blvd.
L-D. *Low*
A good choice for a quick bite between shows is Billy Bob's, where first-rate half-pound burgers, fried pies, and other American diner eats can be accompanied by all sorts of dairy delights.

Billy Gail's Cafe *(417)338-8883*
8 mi. W at 5291 State Hwy. 265
B-L. *Moderate*
Billy Gail's is a blast from the past of rural Ozark Country. A former gas station and rustic country store were transformed many years ago into a down-home coffee shop. Hubcap-sized pancakes, thick French toast and four-egg omelets are features among hearty homestyle fare.

Bradford Inn Eatery BakeShop *(417)338-5555*
7 mi. W at 3590 State Hwy. 265
L only. Closed Sun.–Tues. *Moderate*
bradfordeatery.com
Classic American fare is given skilled attention in light flavorful dishes and updated renditions of grandma's pies and cookies. Don't miss the strawberry-rhubarb pie in season and the chocolate chip cookies anytime. The casual Cape Cod style eatery is enhanced by a panoramic mountain and town view from some tables and a small adjoining dining porch. Bakery items may be available into dinner hours.

Branson Cafe *(417)334-3021*
downtown at 120 W. Main St.
B-L-D. Closed Sun. *Low*
downtownbransoncafe.com
The Branson Cafe has been a local landmark since 1910. Classic country cookin' including delicious homemade desserts like really high lemon meringue pie made this a downtown favorite of residents and travelers alike for more than a

Restaurants

century. The cafe was damaged in the great storm of 2012 but it's now back—and as popular as ever.

Branson Landing
downtown at Branson Landing
L-D.   Moderate
bransonlanding.com
Branson's big pedestrian-friendly shopping-and-dining complex includes numerous large representatives of contemporary dining chains. Each is positioned to have good views above the lake from numerous tables. The **Cantina Laredo** and **Texas Land & Cattle** are best positioned to feature fine close-ups of the awesome water and fire feature on the lake with outdoor seating as well as large interiors. Others bracketing the scene include **Black Oak Grill**, **Joe's Crab Shack**, **Nathan's**, **Old Chicago**, **Garfields** and **Famous Dave's**.

Buckingham's Restaurant & Oasis   *(417)337-7777*
3 mi. W at 2820 W. 76 Country Blvd. (in Clarion Hotel)
D only.   Moderate
clarionhotelbranson.com
Contemporary Continental cuisine is given expert attention in dishes like steak Dianne and venison filet. Tableside cooking, full linen, extensive hand-painted wall murals, and African decor touches contribute to a swanky safari feeling. The adjoining similarly-decorated lounge is outfitted with comfortably overstuffed chairs by picture windows overlooking a courtyard pool and fountain.

Clockers Cafe   *(417)335-2328*
downtown at 103 S. Commercial St.
B-L.   Low
One of the Ozarks' best bargains features old-fashioned all-American home cooking in low-priced, consistently good dishes like three-egg crepe-style omelets with ham and cheddar cheese, or buttermilk biscuits with meat gravy. Warm country decor with booths or highback wood chairs surrounded by memorabilia also appeal to travelers as well as natives.

Restaurants

Crazy Cajun Citchen *(417)338-0621*
11 mi. W at 2820 Indian Point Rd. (at Lakeview Campground)
L-D. Closed Sun.–Mon. Closed Thanksgiving to Apr. 1. Low
crazycajuncitchen.com
The good times roll down by Table Rock Lake. Louisiana cajun and creole classics are authentically rendered in generous portions of assorted gumbos, jambalayas, and etouffes. Do not miss beignets made to order for a memorable conclusion. Mix-and-match tables and chairs and bric-a-brac color the little dining room, plus a popular dining porch.

Ernie Biggs Dueling Pianos *(417)239-3670*
downtown at 505 Branson Landing
L-D.   Moderate
erniebiggs.com
This snazzy nightclub-like cafe features regularly scheduled performances of nonstop stylings from two dueling grand pianos facing each other. Casual fare and drinks are served in this link of a regional chain.

Farmhouse Restaurant *(417)334-9701*
downtown at 119 W. Main
B-L-D.   Low
Nostalgia reigns starting with breakfast where you could get a chicken-fried steak, biscuits and gravy, or grits and all sorts of yesteryear comfort foods that carry through dinner as well. It can all be topped off by blackberry cobbler or apple dumplings. The country theme includes lots of bric-a-brac in the simply cheerful dining room.

Jackie B. Goode's Uptown Cafe *(417)336-3535*
4 mi. W at 285 Highway 165
B-L-D.   Low
Uptown Cafe is a top choice for a combination of good old-fashioned live entertainment served with a casual buffet breakfast. A wide selection for lunch or dinner of all-American comfort foods ranges from country-fried steak and fried pickles to classic soda fountain selections using hand-dipped ice cream. Chrome-and-vinyl diner trim is lavishly done in expansive dining areas overlooking a raised stage. Live vocal and instrumental entertainment is continuous and ever-changing from a broad pool of local talent.

Restaurants

Keeter Center   *(417)239-1900*
4 mi. SW (via US 65) at 1 Opportunity Av. - Point Lookout
L-D. Only brunch on Sun.   *Moderate*
keetercenter.edu
In **William R. Dobyns Dining Room**, New Ozark cuisine achieves the status of a culinary celebration of locally sourced ingredients. To a great extent, the campus itself at College of the Ozarks is the source for most of the ingredients from field to plate. The culinary talent here has expanded worldwide ingredients to include more and more that are produced on-site using new-style greenhouses and hydroponics. Classic Ozark ingredients like pork, apple butter, and green tomatoes become extraordinary twenty-first-century dishes that emphasize flavors in lighter livelier styles. Careful attention to details and local sourcing are even reflected in the baked goods using flour milled on campus. Don't miss the hickory-smoked tomato soup with basil cream, and fried green tomatoes with a skiff of homemade jalapeño jelly. Additionally, on-campus dairy animals are used to produce both fine cheeses and unusual ice creams and sorbets like blueberry basil. Apiary supplies are now sourced on campus for assorted honey products. Seasonally fresh local fruits are featured in desserts like strawberry-rhubarb cobbler. Sunday brunch is a popular showcase for their talents, and outdoor seating is delightful when weather permits. The big stylish wood-trimmed dining room has comfortably padded craft-hewn chairs and solid polished tables, hardwood floors, stamped-metal ceiling, and fresh flowers and fine napery on each table. A frequently played grand piano, raised fireplace, and a window wall view of the Ozarks complete the charming setting. Delicious breakfast pastries are also available every morning. The new **Nettie Marie's Creamery** offers delectable homemade ice cream flavors by the scoop in the lobby.

Level 2 Steakhouse   *(417) 243-3433*
downtown in Hilton at 200 E. Main St.
B-L-D.   *Very Expensive*
level2steakhouse.com
Branson's landmark convention hotel at the Landing offers fine dining in Level 2. Steaks like filet mignon, Wagyu, or bison ribeye star on a contemporary American cuisine with many choices of sauces, toppings and sides to complement premium

Restaurants

cuts of meat. Housemade desserts top off the experience. All meals are served in plush dining areas featuring full linen.
Ma's Place   *(417)739-4228*
17 mi. W at 13317 State Highway 13 - Kimberling City
B-L.   *Low*
For budget-oriented classic Southern road food, there's Ma's. This freestanding coffee shop is on a rise high above Table Rock Lake. Abundant Southern comfort food like biscuits and sausage gravy, specialty pancakes, tasty crepe-style omelets, cinnamon rolls, and more are served at breakfast. Lunch options are similarly diverse, topped off by assorted pies and fruit cobblers. Several bright and tidy little dining areas are in keeping with the coffee shop's name.
Mel's Hard Luck Diner   *(417)332-0150*
3 mi. W at 2800 W. 76 Country Blvd.
L-D.   *Moderate*
restaurantsbransonmo.com
This classic 50's style diner has a special feature—the whole staff takes turns at the mike singing their favorites ranging from 50's and 60's pop classics through country/western to Broadway and movie tunes. And, they can be very good. Their interaction with the audience is inevitably appealing. So, everyone has fun, and the food is as all-American as the staff's passion for enjoying this as a showcase for their talent. Retro food like a root beer malt goes well with the native entertainment.
Mr. Gilberti's Place   *(417)334-9322*
5 mi. SW at 1451 Acacia Club Rd. - Hollister
L-D.   *Moderate*
mrgilbertis.com
Authentic Chicago style pizza based on the owner's family recipes has made this a favorite for pizza in the region. The dough is prepared daily, along with all sauces, spices and sausage for pizzas that can be garnished with more than a dozen different toppings. Soups, salads, sandwiches and pasta classics are also served, along with spumoni, gelato and cannoli for dessert. A transformed roadside house includes comfortable little dining areas that look and smell right for Chicago-style Italian dining.

Restaurants

Mitsu Neko Fusion Cuisine *(417)336-1819*
2 mi. W at 1819 W. Hwy 76, Suite D
L-D.   *Moderate*
Tucked away in a little complex by the main entertainment street is a contemporary Japanese restaurant featuring "fusion cuisine" ranging from seared salmon to potstickers and shrimp tempuras and other classic and creative cooked dishes. A dozen tables in a simply stylish dining room are backed by an expo sushi bar.

Outback Steak & Oyster Bar *(417)334-6306*
2 mi. W at 1914 W. 76 Country Blvd.
L-D.   *Moderate*
outbackbranson.com
The Outback is a long-established dining adventure. Try a gator tail appetizer. Hearty portions, abundant Outback Australian decor in numerous dining areas and bar, an expo grill, and shady dining verandas distinguish this expansive complex.

Rocky's Italian Restaurant *(417)335-4765*
downtown at 120 N. Sycamore St.
L-D.   *Moderate*
Generous portions of flavorful Southern Italian classics like lasagna or cannelloni, or veal marsala or scampi, are featured on an extensive menu. Comfortable wood-trimmed dining areas with a choice of padded booths or chairs provide a warm, relaxed setting in a transformed turn-of-the-century feed mill outfitted with distinctive local wall art.

The Shack Cafe *(417)334-3490*
downtown at 108 S. Commercial St.
B-L.   *Low*
The Shack is one of the big four old-time Ozark-style coffee shops. All serve abundant all-American comfort food that have long drawn crowds of natives and tourists to the heart of Branson. The Shack's distinction is their housemade pies. Mile-high meringue is taken to new heights in tasty lemon, coconut, or chocolate pie crowned by a mound of some of the finest meringue anywhere—six inches of it.

Restaurants

Table 22   *(417) 973-0022*
downtown at 114 E Main St.
D only.   *Very Expensive*
table22branson.com

Cutting-edge cuisine has arrived in Branson. Combinations of fresh ingredients are intended to surprise and delight diners with their unusual appearance, flavors and textures. Sometimes the talented chef's results are stellar like a soup that is transformed before your eyes from an unassuming pile into a delectable taste sensation. However, some offerings on the ever-changing menu fall short of expectations, so diners may disagree on whether this is a new sensation or a one-time experience. The small avant-garde dining room keeps focus on the cuisine and its presentation.

White River Fish House   *(417)243-5100*
downtown at 1 Bass Pro Dr. at Branson Landing
L-D.   *Moderate*
whiteriverfishhouse.com

The White River Fish House is a delightful destination for Ozark and Southern specialties. Consider an alligator tail appetizer or venison-stuffed mushrooms, an Ozark catfish fry, or pan-fried trout almondine, buffalo burger, or fall-off-the-bone barbecue ribs. All are skillfully prepared and artfully served. There is also a wealth of soups, salads, and sandwiches. Appealing desserts made here include a bodaciously bountiful fruit cobbler served in a skillet. The big restaurant is full of fish-camp-themed Ozark arts crafts and taxidermy. It actually floats on Lake Taneycomo adjacent to the promenade and landing, within sight of the fabulous fountain.

LODGINGS

Accommodations are superabundant in and around town. Most are moderately priced, and range from plush resorts by the lakes to large hotels and motels near the theaters. Late spring through early fall is prime time. Winter rates are often reduced 40% or more.

All American Inn & Suites *(417)334-2800   (866)919-2284*
4 mi. SW at 3102 Falls Pkwy. - 65616
81 units   *Moderate*
allamericaninnandsuites.com

The All American Inn & Suites is a recently refurbished three-story complex on the quiet side of the 76 Strip. Amenities include a view pool and expanded Continental breakfast, plus cookies in the afternoon. Rooms are well furnished with a refrigerator and microwave. Suites also have an in-room two-person whirlpool.

Big Cedar Lodge   *(417)335-2777   (800)225-6343*
10 mi. SW at 612 Devil's Pool Rd. - Ridgedale 65739
247 units   *Expensive–Very Expensive*
bigcedar.com

Big Cedar Lodge is the Ozarks' premier resort with a wealth of activities and amenities. Deep in lush forested hills by picturesque Table Rock Lake (with 43,000 acres of water), the complex is both rustic and majestic. Richly grained woods and rough stone distinguish dozens of buildings up to four stories surrounded by expansive grounds that look natural rather than manicured, accented with ponds and waterfalls, wooden bridges and stone paths. Functional whimsical sculptures abound. Amenities include use of **Brushy Creek Clubhouse at the Wilderness Club** with an indoor pool and (in summer) an outdoor swimming pool with whirlpool, and as their main attraction, a scenic lazy river. There is also a marina for registered guests with dockage for your boat plus all sorts of boat rentals, ski and pontoon boats. Canoes are complimentary. Elsewhere on-site are stables with horseback riding and carriage rides; mini-golf course, pro shop, jogging, nature, and hiking trails; large view pool, whirlpool, two spas offering a wealth of wellness and beauty treatments (see listing), lakeview sand volleyball court and shuffleboard courts; idyllic fine dining (see listing), and atmospheric lounges. Unusual specialty activities include

Lodgings

campfire wagon tours. The nine-hole **Top of the Rock Golf Course** designed by Jack Nicklaus and Arnold Palmer features real challenges and spectacular views of Table Rock Lake. There is an elaborate practice facility with 18 greens, a lovely putting green, and a grand view restaurant and lounge. A golf learning center and pro shop complete the golfing experience. The elaborate Fitness Center is newly upgraded with elaborate machines for strength and aerobics and a personal trainer is available, plus a sauna, pool and three terraced whirlpools with outstanding lake views. There is a resort shop full of local products, souvenirs and travel-oriented gifts. The on-site conference center is one of America's most satisfying marriages of grand architecture, inspired decor and spectacular setting. Quality artwork, crafts and antiques are used throughout. Additional features include state-of-the-art **Ancient History Museum of the Ozarks**; **Chapel of the Ozarks** overlooking Table Rock Lake, and visit caves including the unique **Cave Bar** along the **Lost Canyon Nature Trail**. Lodgings scattered around the well-spaced buildings include luxuriously furnished rooms that capture the spirit of the Ozark wilderness. All rooms have been fully renovated recently. Many romantic knotty pine cabins have a large private lake-view deck, plus a two-person whirlpool and stone fireplace. The newest lodging units (Falls Lodge) crown a ridge with balconies overlooking panoramic views of the lake, a whirlpool bath, gas fireplace and their signature wildlife-themed decor. Most units have a refrigerator and microwave. Each cabin has a kitchen and comes stocked with a basket of goodies. As a final bonus, all units are visited by the cookie lady every evening.

Bradford House   *(417)334-4444   (888)488-4445*
5 mi. SW at 296 Blue Meadows Rd. - 65616
20 units   *Moderate*
bradfordhouse.us

Bradford House is a large three-story Victorian-mansion-style building outfitted with an extensive collection of antique and reproduction furnishings. Amenities include a pool with a forest view and full breakfast. Each room is attractively furnished with the Victorian theme, and several have an in-bath whirlpool. "Forever Yours" has half-circular windows and a two-person whirlpool, while "Carissa's Choice" is a cheerful corner room with many windows.

Lodgings

Bradford Inn   *(417)338-5555   (800)357-1466*
7 mi. W at 3590 State Hwy. 265 - 65616
34 units   Moderate
bradfordinn.us
Topping a tranquil ridge to the west of Branson's action is the Bradford Inn. Many windows capture delightful views of town and the Ozark Hill Country. Buffet breakfast is complimentary, including fresh baked goods. Each well-furnished, spacious room has a private deck or patio that shares the view. Some rooms also have a raised gas fireplace and/or two-person whirlpool and refrigerator.

Branson Towers Hotel   *(417)336-4500*
3 mi. NW at 236 Shepherd of the Hills
200 units   Moderate
bransontowers.com
This large contemporary motel tops a hill above the northern bypass of the entertainment district. Amenities include a large indoor pool and whirlpool. Hot buffet breakfast is complimentary, and there is a (fee) ice cream social hour. Each room is comfortably furnished, and some have a whirlpool tub.

Branson's Best   *(417)336-2378   (800)404-5013*
4 mi. W (via W. 76 Blvd.) at 3150 Green Mountain Rd. - 65616
66 units   Low
bransonsbest.com
Here is competition for the best deal in town. Amenities include a kidney-shaped pool in a quiet corner backed by a forest. Expanded Continental breakfast includes biscuits and gravy, sausage patties and waffles. In the evening free ice cream, cobbler and cookies are featured. Each well-furnished room includes a refrigerator. One unit has a town view and a two-person whirlpool.

Castle Rock Resort/Waterpark   *(417)336-6000 (888)273-3919*
4 mi. W at 3001 Green Mountain Dr. - 65616
200 units   Moderate–Expensive
castlerockbranson.com
The tower features a (fee) 30,000 square foot indoor waterpark with two major slides and a small "lazy river." There are also related water features outdoors, a restaurant and lounge, gift shop, day spa, and game room with air hockey. Expanded Continental breakfast is available for a fee. There are family-oriented comfortably furnished rooms in the Tower. Across a parking lot, a few units have an in-room two-person whirlpool.

Lodgings

Center Pointe Inn - Best Western *(417)334-1894 (877)334-1894*
4 mi. W at 3215 W. 76 Country Blvd. - 65616
164 units   Moderate
bransonbestwesterns.com/branson-lodging.htm
In the heart of the entertainment district, this large modern motel offers an indoor and outdoor pool, whirlpool, sauna, exercise room, game room and expanded Continental breakfast. Rooms are comfortably furnished.

Chateau on the Lake Resort Spa & Convention Center
(417)334-1161   (888)333-5253
9 mi. SW at 415 N. State Hwy. 265 - 65616
301 units   Expensive–Very Expensive
chateauonthelake.com
High on a hill overlooking Table Rock is a chateau-style hotel with a full-service 14,000-square-foot spa including an infinity pool that is filled from the ceiling and an outdoor lakeview Roman bath beneath a waterfall; indoor and outdoor pools and whirlpools; a nearby marina with all sorts of rental boats and gear (canoes, kayaks and paddleboats); fitness center and tennis courts; and a nature trail; plus **Chateau Grille** (B-L-D—Very Expensive) and lounge with a distant lake view and fireplace, a sweets shop, cafe and deli. Rooms are beautifully furnished. Some suites include a whirlpool bathtub and a small lake-view balcony.

Clarion Hotel at the Palace   *(417)334-7666   (800)725-2236*
3 mi. W at 2820 W. 76 Country Blvd. - 65616
166 units   Moderate–Expensive
clarionhotelbranson.com
This hotel is in the midst of the entertainment strip. Theaters are a stroll from the attractive contemporary seven-story complex with two pools (one indoor), whirlpools, sauna, exercise room, two restaurants (see **Buckingham's**) and lounge, and complimentary expanded Continental breakfast. Each well-furnished room has a private view balcony. Some also have a whirlpool bath.

Comfort Inn & Suites   *(417)335-4731   (877)746-8357*
3 mi. NW at 5150 N. Gretna Rd. - 65616
121 units   Moderate
comfortinn.com
This four-story complex on a quiet side of town has a large indoor saltwater pool, whirlpool, sauna, exercise room, game

Lodgings

room, and complimentary expanded Continental breakfast. Each room is well furnished. Suites also have a refrigerator and microwave. Two extra-large units also have a two-person whirlpool tub in the bedroom.

Grand Country Inn *(417)335-3535   (888)514-1088*
2 mi. W at 1945 W. 76 Country Blvd. - 65616
319 units   *Moderate*
grandcountry.com
Grand Country Inn is ideally suited for parents with children. The area's original indoor waterpark features two tube slides, a tall combination climbing and dunking tower, a small lazy river, and two whirlpools. The outdoor waterpark has a slide, pool and interactive waterplay. There is also a (fee) fun spot with laser tag, mini-golf, mini-bowling, bumper cars and a play area, plus shops and a grill. All of the family-oriented rooms are comfortably furnished.

Hilton Branson Convention Ctr *(417)336-5400 (800)445-8667*
downtown at 200 E. Main St. - 65616
292 units   *Expensive*
bransonconventioncenter.hilton.com
Hilton's major convention-oriented hotel opened in 2007. The twelve-story complex has an outstanding location adjacent to downtown one way and the Landing and Lake Taneycomo the other. It is connected to the stylish Convention Center a short stroll from Branson's world class fire-and-water-jets fountain. Amenities include an indoor and large outdoor pool; whirlpools; fitness center; fine dining at **Level 2 Steakhouse** (see listing), and a comfortable lounge. Rooms are thoroughly contemporary, beautifully furnished and include refrigerators. Some have outstanding downtown and waterfront views.

Hilton Promenade at Branson Landing
(417)336-5500   (800)445-8667
downtown at 3 Branson Landing Blvd. - 65616
243 units   *Expensive*
hilton.com
The Hilton Promenade is the centerpiece for the massive transformation of Branson's downtown waterfront. Adjacent to the world-class fire-and-water-jets fountain synchronized to music, the complex is also at the intersection of the main street to the historic downtown and the pedestrian boulevard that extends the length of the blocks-long post-millennium

Lodgings

commercial center at Branson Landing by Lake Taneycomo. An indoor pool, whirlpool and exercise room are other amenities, along with a restaurant and lounge. Each unit in the au courant six-story complex is beautifully furnished and includes a mini-refrigerator. Many have a direct window outlook to the riverside plaza's fabulous three-hundred-foot-long fountain cantilevered along Lake Taneycomo. One-, two- and three-bedroom view condos are also available.

Hotel Grand Victorian *(417)336-2935* *(800)324-8751*
3 mi. W at 2325 W. 76 Country Blvd. - 65616
151 units   Moderate–Expensive
hotelgrandvictorian.com

This handsome five-story motel has a large indoor and an outdoor pool, whirlpool, exercise room and game room with a pool table. An expanded Continental breakfast is complimentary as are afternoon treats. Each well-furnished room is themed appropriately to the property's name. Many rooms have a small private balcony overlooking the 76 Strip or a fine backcountry view, and a whirlpool tub. All rooms have a refrigerator. Many beautifully furnished suites on the top floor have a raised two-person whirlpool.

Keeter Center *(417)239-1900*
4 mi. SW at 1 Opportunity Av. - Point Lookout 65726
15 units   Expensive
keetercenter.edu

The Keeter Center is the tranquil showplace of the captivating College of the Ozarks. All facilities on the campus of "Hard Work U" are operated by students. This twenty-first-century rustic wood-trim building displays the timeless charm of the Ozarks. Massive lodgepoles, polished hardwood floors, large raised fireplaces of native stone, and rustic wood and leather-trimmed furniture distinguish interiors that include a dramatic four-story lobby, a gift nook featuring College-made products, and an expansive dining room (see listing) with campus and Hill Country views. **Mabee Lodge** rooms all feature a kitchen, fireplace, and oversize private balcony. Suites feature complimentary in-room Continental breakfast, evening cookies and farm-fresh College of the Ozarks milk. For romantic accommodations, the beautifully furnished Loft Suites with vaulted ceilings and fine views are tops and include a two-person whirlpool.

Lodgings

Lodge of the Ozarks   *(417)334-7535   (877)327-9894*
4 mi. W at 3431 W. 76 Country Blvd. - 65616
186 units   Moderate
lodgeoftheozarks.com
The Lodge of the Ozarks is both well located for action and attractively themed to the Hill Country. Amenities include a large indoor pool, whirlpool, exercise rooms, meeting rooms, restaurant and complimentary Continental breakfast. Well-furnished rooms range from standard to king suites with an in-bath two-person whirlpool. Some have a refrigerator.

Radisson Hotel Branson   *(417)335-5767   (800)333-3333*
3 mi. W (via W. 76 Blvd.) at 120 S. Wildwood Dr. - 65616
472 units   Moderate–Expensive
radissonbranson.com
Branson's biggest hotel is in the heart of the theater district. Amenities in the contemporary ten-story complex include an indoor/outdoor pool, whirlpool, sauna, exercise room, restaurant, lounge, and meeting facilities. Each recently renovated room is attractively furnished. Well-furnished spacious suites on the ninth floor feature a private standing balcony with a wide-angle town view, and a two-person whirlpool bath.

Rock Lane Resort & Marina   *(417)338-2211   (800)762-5526*
11 mi. W (via Indian Point Rd.) at 611 Rock Lane Rd. - 65616
40 units   Moderate
rocklane.com
Rock Lane Resort is a big contemporary motel/condominium complex sprawled along a little peninsula by Table Rock Lake. Amenities include a full-service public marina with rentals for everything from pontoon boats to jet skis; lake cruises; two pools; a tennis court; covered fishing dock; and game facilities including pool tables. **Charlie's** (L-D—Moderate) offers food and drinks with picture-window lake views. Well-furnished motel rooms have a refrigerator, microwave, and a private balcony, many with a lake overlook. One- to three-bedroom condominiums are Moderate to Expensive. Many have fine lake views and a refrigerator and microwave.

Lodgings

Savannah House Hotel *(417)336-3132   (800)383-3132*
3 mi. NW at 165 Expressway Lane - 65616
165 units   Low–Moderate
savannahhousebranson.com
Competition for the best bargain in Branson is the Savannah House. The large good-looking three-story post-millennium hotel is high on a hill above the major bypass west of downtown with a panoramic view of surrounding Ozark highlights. In addition to a pool, whirlpool and fitness room, they offer a full breakfast in a comfortably outfitted dining/relaxation area, plus ice cream, cobbler, and cookies every evening along with a 24-hour coffee/cappuccino machine. Each room is well furnished and has a refrigerator. Some have a fine view. There are several suites with a whirlpool in the room.

Scenic Hills Inn   *(417)336-8855   (888)800-5577*
3 mi. W at 2422 Shepherd of the Hills Expressway - 65616
66 units   Low
scenichillsinn.com
A small pool and whirlpool distinguish this motel set back from the main bypass highway in a quiet location. An expanded Continental breakfast includes warm dishes (biscuits and gravy, waffles, french toast, and homemade cinnamon rolls). Each comfortably furnished room includes all contemporary amenities and a refrigerator.

Still Waters Lakefront Resort *(417)338-2323   (800)777-2320*
11 mi. W at 21 Stillwater Trail - 65616
238 units   Expensive
stillwatersresort.com
Still Waters is the most complete lakefront resort in the region. Sprawled along a peninsula in a forest are numerous units in four-story buildings ranging from standard motel rooms to four-bedroom condominiums. Facilities include boats and jet ski rentals, free use of paddleboats, inner tubes and kayaks; and there are designated swimming areas in the lake, plus three freeform pools, one with a swell swim-under waterfall area. There are also free bikes, a short waterslide, a large whirlpool, plus a market, deli and gift shop. Most well-furnished units (from standard rooms to four-bedroom condos) have private balconies with a fine lake view through trees. Some units also have a two-person whirlpool.

Lodgings
The Stone Castle Hotel & Conference Center
(417)335-4700   (800)677-6906
4 mi. W (via W. 76 Blvd.) at 3050 Green Mountain Dr.
- 65616
299 units   Low–Moderate
bransonstonecastle.com
Competition for the best bargain and the largest lodging in town is the Stone Castle Hotel, a four-story themed complex that sprawls along a hill in a quiet section near the entertainment strip. Amenities include two indoor pools and two whirlpools, a game room with air hockey, and a complimentary expanded Continental breakfast. In addition to standard motel rooms, thirty-seven whirlpool theme rooms star with a private balcony, large in-room whirlpool, refrigerator, microwave, and creative fun themed decor ranging from Taj Mahal to Sherlock Holmes.

Welk Resort Branson   *(417)336-3575   (800)505-9355*
7 mi. SW at 1984 State Hwy. 165 - 65616
160 units   Moderate–Expensive
welkresortbranson.com
The Welk Resort Branson features a "splashatorium" with one major slide and a large indoor pool and hot tub plus an outdoor pool. There is also a large fitness center and game room, miniature golf, restaurant, lounge, and a large live theater with occasional big name performances. Hot breakfast can be purchased for a fee. Each recently renovated room is well furnished.

White River Lodge   *(417)779-1556   (800)544-0257*
16 mi. SW at 738 Ozark Hollow Rd. - Blue Eye 65611
5 units   Expensive
whiteriverlodge.com
White River Lodge is one of America's most romantic adult getaways. Nestled in a lush deciduous forest high on a hill overlooking Table Rock Lake is a bed-and-breakfast that perfectly epitomizes the warm charm of the Ozarks. Fir and pine in everything from rough-hewn logs to polished fittings and Arkansas fieldstone are showcased in a wilderness-style mansion that was completed in 2005 to serve as a bed-and-breakfast. Amenities include a large flagstone patio and whirlpool with a panoramic lake view; fitness and game center including ping pong and billiards; sauna/steam room;

Lodgings

theater room; common area kitchen, barbecue, refrigerator, and wet bar for guest use; and covered parking. As a key added attraction, the owner is a licensed guide who has hosted fishing trips on the famed local chain of lakes for more than twenty years. Delicious breakfast is complimentary along with afternoon refreshments. Every extra-large room includes a raised gas fireplace, a whirlpool tub, and private view deck or balcony. Each room is luxuriously appointed with Ozark-style arts, antiques and artifacts housed amidst wood trim ranging from rough logs to polished fittings. Two rooms ("Couples Cove" and "Foggy River") have a king bed with an intimate view of a two-person whirlpool tub, raised gas fireplace as well as picture windows with panoramic forest and lake views.

BASIC INFORMATION

Elevation: 722 feet Population (2010): 10,520
Location: 210 miles South of Kansas City, MO
Nearest airport with commercial flights: in town
Branson/Lakes Area Chamber of Commerce/CVB
  (417)334-4084   (800)296-0463
  1 mi. N (near US 65) at 269 Hwy. 248 (Box 1897) - 65615
  explorebranson.com

LIVABILITY

The preceding listings have all the information you need to translate your ideas and dreams into a fun-filled vacation. But, suppose you fall in love with Branson after a memorable visit. What if you decide you want to live there?

Data for six key indicators are described below that can affect people's hometown choice. Uniform national statistics were compiled from the 2010 federal census, 2010–12 FBI data, historic weather data, and private data sources. All data relate to in-town boundaries except presidential voting data which is at the county level.

Livability Indicators

Weather. Weather affects usability of the alluring surroundings of a great town, and can make or break a vacation if you're into outdoor sports, photography, or even strolling in town. The Vokac Weather Rating © graph reflects the probability, on a scale of zero to ten, of warm, dry fully usable "shirt-sleeve" weather. The weather score is the average Vokac Weather Rating for the year (derived from detailed monthly weather data for each town). Branson ranks 50th among America's hundred great towns. With a composite rating of 4.3, it is above the nation as a whole, but not to the point that people would relocate here for a mild climate.

Education. Branson ranked 63nd of the 100 great towns for attainment of a high school diploma. With 89% of Branson residents reporting a high school diploma, it exceeds the nation as a whole at 85%. However, the nation reports a somewhat higher attainment of a college degree (28% compared to Branson's 24%). This puts Branson in the midrange of education.

Crime. Crime statistics are misleading for Branson. Data suggest the rate of violent crime in Branson is significantly higher than that of the nation as a whole. However, the reported per-capita rate is skewed by the fact that the town houses millions of additional visitors each year at a much

Livability

higher visitor-to-resident ratio than most towns. Another factor is the higher-than-typical staffing level of law enforcement officers intent on assuring that all criminal behavior gets reported and acted upon. While care should be taken in any locale where a large tourist population is present, Branson is not considered a high crime district by residents or most visitors.

Income. Branson ranks 67th among the hundred great towns with a $51,538 median household income in 2010, which is below the U.S.A. average of $52,762. Both median family income and per capita income were similarly ranked. Happily, it is offset by reasonable housing costs.

Housing. Everyone is concerned about the cost of housing—its value if you are an owner; its cost if you are a buyer or renter. Branson ranked 13th for housing affordability among the hundred towns at $174,000 at a time when the national average was $186,000 Its rank on rent affordability was #22, with a rent cost only 83% of the national average.

Politics. The political leanings of a community may or may not impact a person's satisfaction with living in a locale. Some towns comfortably support a wide diversity of opinions, while others clearly favor a political viewpoint. Branson is the seventh most conservative of the 100 great towns. Many of the live shows celebrate traditional American family values, and it continues to appeal to families and individuals imbued with the historic American spirit established in the Constitution and the Bill of Rights.

Ongoing Research
While the indicators described above are not all-inclusive, they do suggest town characteristics that may influence your decision on whether you would enjoy living in Branson. If you would like more information, visit ***greattowns.com***. That website dedicated to all of America's best getaways beyond the cities includes an evolving presentation of relevant livability indicators as a key feature.

ABOUT THE AUTHORS

David Vokac was born in Chicago and grew up on a ranch near Cody, Wyoming. He served as the first airborne fire-spotter for the Shoshone National Forest next to Yellowstone National Park. Later, he taught land economics while completing a Masters degree in geography at the University of Arizona. In Denver, David headed the City's economic base analysis and the Neighborhood Planning division. He moved to Southern California in 1974 to direct San Diego County's local parks program. David is the author of seventeen (hard copy) guidebooks, including the acclaimed **Great Towns of America** series.

Joan Vokac was born and raised in New Jersey. She earned a Bachelors degree from Bucknell University and a Masters at the University of Michigan. She worked as a land use planner for the unincorporated towns in San Diego County for thirty years. Joan is now a full-time travel writer and also serves as the webmaster for the site that supports this guidebook—***www.greattowns.com***.

To keep apprised of the Vokacs' travels, to add comments and suggestions regarding their work, for continuing updates on America's top getaways, and to find out about upcoming titles, visit *www.greattowns.com* and *facebook.com/greattowns*.

INDEX

All American Inn & Suites   30
Ancient History Museum of the Ozarks   31
Andy's Frozen Custard   22
Attractions   12–21
Basic Information   39
Big Cedar Lodge - restaurants   22–23
Big Cedar Lodge - lodgings   30–31
Big Cedar Spa   18
Billy Bob Dairyland   23
Billy Gail's Cafe   23
Black Oak Grill   24
Boat Rentals   12
Boat Rides   12
Bradford House   31
Bradford Inn   32
Bradford Inn Eatery BakeShop   23
Branson Cafe   23–24
Branson/Lakes Area Chamber of Commerce   39
Branson Landing   24
Branson Scenic Railway   12–13
Branson Towers Hotel   32
Branson Zipline and Canopy Tours   20
Branson's Best   32
Brushy Creek Clubhouse at Wilderness Club   30
Buckingham's Restaurant & Oasis   24
Butterfly Palace   13
Buzzards Bar   23
Cantina Laredo   24
Canyon Cafe   14
Castle Rock Resort & Waterpark   32
Cave Bar   31
Center Pointe Inn - Best Western   33
Chapel of the Ozarks   31
Charlie's   36
Chateau Grille   33
Chateau on the Lake Resort Spa & Convention Center   33
Clarion Hotel at the Palace   33
Clockers Cafe   24
College of the Ozarks - college   13
College of the Ozards - Food Specialties   15
College of the Ozarks - Lodging   35–36
College of the Ozarks - Restaurant   26
Comfort Inn & Suites   33–34
Crazy Cajun Citchen   25

Index

Devil's Pool Restaurant 22
Dobyn's 26
Dogwood Canyon Nature Park 13–14
Downtown 14
Ernie Biggs Dueling Piano 25
Extreme Racing Center 20
Famous Dave's 24
Farmhouse Restaurant 25
Food Specialties 14
Fountain at Lake Taneycomo 15
Garfields 24
Grand Country Inn 34
Hilton Branson Convention Center 34
Hilton Promenade at Branson Landing 34–35
History 10
Hotel Grand Victorian 35
Indian Point 15
Indian Point Zipline Adventure Tours 20
Jackie B. Goode's Uptown Cafe 25
Joe's Crab Shack 24
Kayak Branson 12
Keeter Center - lodging 35
Keeter Center - restaurant 26
Lake Taneycomo 15
Level 2 Steakhouse 26–27
Livability 40–41
Live Theater 15–16
Lodge of the Ozarks 36
Lodgings 30–39
Lost Canyon Nature Trail 31
Ma's Place 27
Mabee Lodge 35
Main Street Lake Cruises 12
Mark Twain National Forest 16–17
Marvel Cave 18
Mel's Hard Luck Diner 27
Mr. Gilberti's Place 27
Mitsu Neko Fusion Cuisine 28
Nathan's 24
Nettie Marie's Creamery 26
Old Chicago 24
Outback Steak & Oyster Bar 28
Radisson Hotel Branson 36
Ralph Foster Museum 13
Restaurants 22–29

Index

Ride the Ducks   17
Rock Lane Resort & Marina   36
Rocky's Italian Restaurant   28
Savannah House Hotel   37
Scenic Hills Inn   37
Shack Cafe   28
Shepherd of the Hills   17
Shoji Tabuchi   16
Showboat Branson Belle   17
Silver Dollar City   17–18
Smirnoff, Yakov   16
Spa   18
Still Waters Lakefront Resort   37
Stone Castle Hotel & Conference Center   38
Table 22   29
Table Rock Lake Pontoon Rentals   12
Table Rock Lake State Park   18
Tabuchi, Shoji   16
Talking Rocks Cavern   19
Texas Land & Cattle   24
Titanic   19
Top of the Rock Golf Course   31
Top of the Rock Restaurant   23
Truman Coffee & Cafe   22
Veterans Memorial Museum   19
Vigilante Extreme ZipRider   20–21
Warm Water Features   19
Weather   11
Welk Resort Branson   38
White River Fish House   29
White River Lodge   38–39
White Water   19
William R. Dobyns Dining Room   26
Wings of the World   19
Worman House   22–23
Yakov Smirnoff   16
Zip Line USA   21
Ziplines   20–21